The Ultimate
ORIGAMI
Book

20 Projects and **184 Pages**
of Super Cool Craft Paper

FOX CHAPEL
PUBLISHING

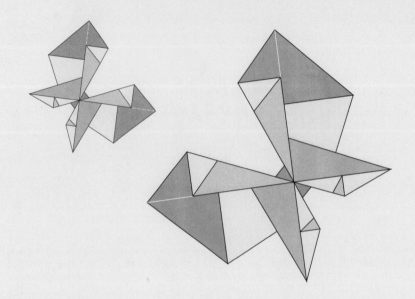

ISBN 978-1-4971-0125-8

Cataloging-in-Publication data is on file with the Library of Congress.

To learn more about the other great books from Fox Chapel Publishing, or to find a retailer near
you, call toll-free 800-457-9112 or visit us at *www.FoxChapelPublishing.com*.

We are always looking for talented authors. To submit an idea, please send a brief inquiry to
acquisitions@foxchapelpublishing.com.

Printed in China
First printing

In this book, you'll discover the amazing world of Japanese origami. By folding a lotus flower, a delicate crane, a sumo wrestler, a school of little fish, and more, you'll get to explore fun paper-folding projects from the Land of the Rising Sun!

Thanks to the clear diagrams and explanations that accompany every project, you will have no trouble making these elegant folded items. Fold multiples of your favorites to create mobiles, garlands, and hanging decorations. And why not gift some of your finished work to others? Whether in your home or the home of a friend, these origami projects make superb décor pieces.

Choose one of the many sheets of paper in this book and get folding. Don't hesitate to fold the same project several times, and don't be afraid to try things out, restart if you make a mistake, and learn as you go. You'll soon feel the satisfaction of being able to say, "I made that!"

Very easy   Easy   Intermediate

Contents

Folds and Symbols

Before getting started, review these pages well in order to familiarize yourself with the symbols and markings that are used throughout the instructions in this book. They will tell you how to fold the paper at each step.

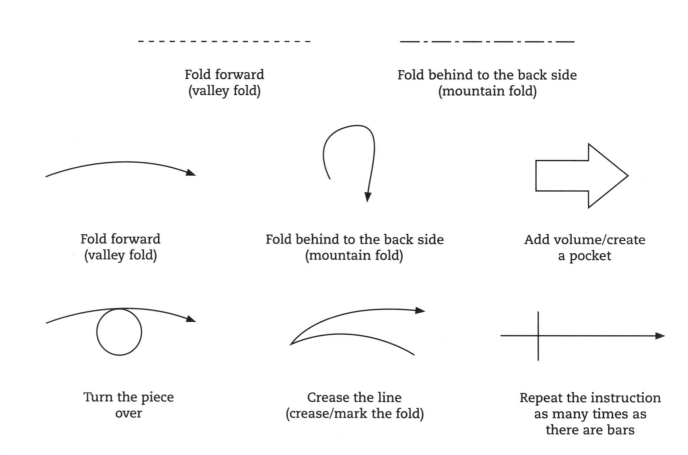

Fold forward
(valley fold)

Fold behind to the back side
(mountain fold)

Fold forward
(valley fold)

Fold behind to the back side
(mountain fold)

Add volume/create
a pocket

Turn the piece
over

Crease the line
(crease/mark the fold)

Repeat the instruction
as many times as
there are bars

The following basic folds, as displayed on the paper illustrations for each step, will be frequently used.

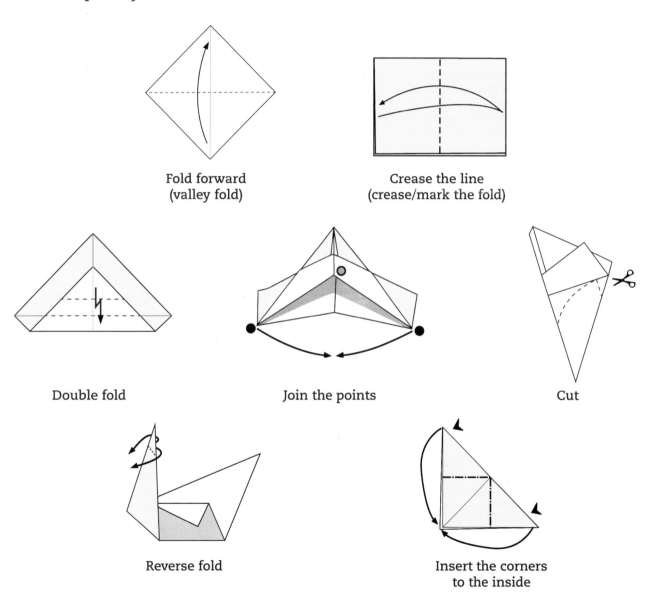

Fold forward
(valley fold)

Crease the line
(crease/mark the fold)

Double fold

Join the points

Cut

Reverse fold

Insert the corners
to the inside

Delicate Crane

This flying bird makes a great garland or mobile. It's a classic and essential piece of origami!

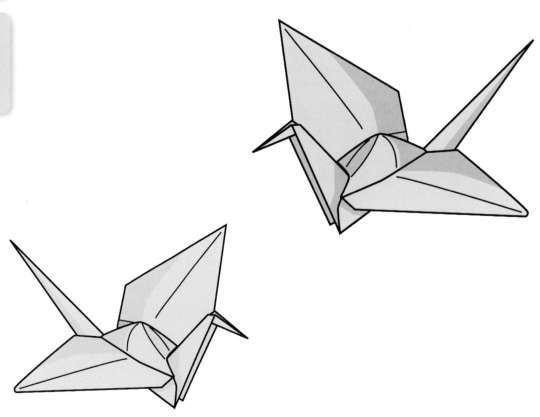

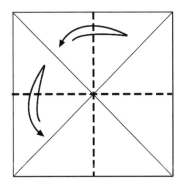

1 Crease the lines as shown.

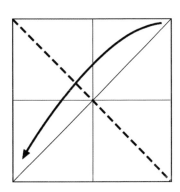

2 Fold diagonally.

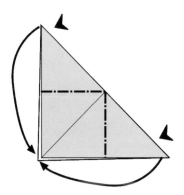

3 Insert the corners to the inside.

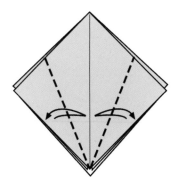

4 Turn the piece so that the opening is at the bottom. Crease the lines as shown.

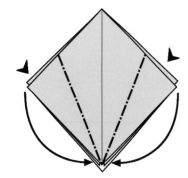

5 On the front side, insert the corners to the inside as in step 3.

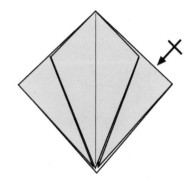

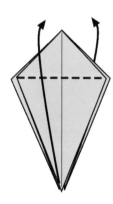

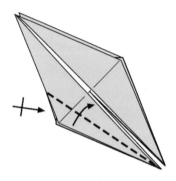

6 Repeat steps 4 and 5 on the back side.

7 Fold up the points on both the front and back sides.

8 Fold in the left side on both the front and back sides.

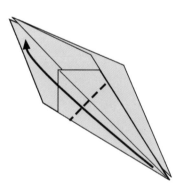

9 Open and press flat the left side.

10 Fold up the point.

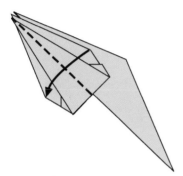

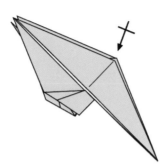

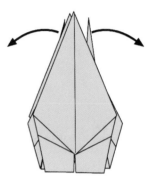

11 Fold in half.

12 Repeat steps 8–11 on the right side.

13 Gently pull out the interior points.

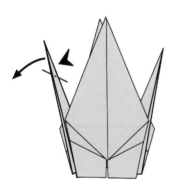

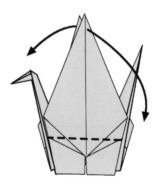

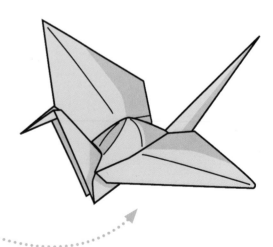

14 For the head, fold the tip and then reverse the fold.

15 Lower the wings on each side.

Mount Fuji

MATERIAL
- 1 sheet

**COLOR
SUGGESTIONS**

What is a more iconic landmark in Japan than Mount Fuji? This is an easy project for creating the famous mountain.

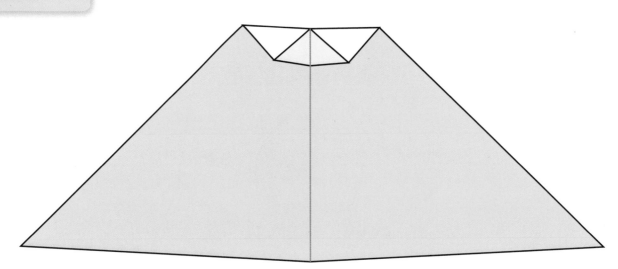

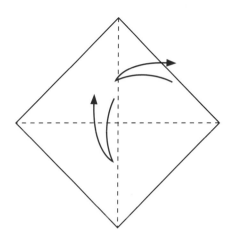

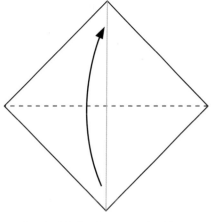

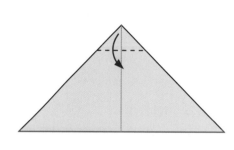

1 Crease the lines as shown.

2 Fold the bottom half up.

3 Fold down the tip on the front side.

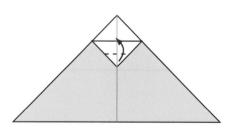

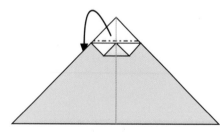

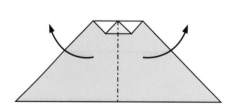

4 Fold up the very tip of the tip.

5 Fold down the tip behind to the back side.

6 Lightly fold to form the standing shape.

Little Boat

MATERIAL
- 1 sheet

COLOR SUGGESTIONS

This is a truly charming traditional Japanese vessel that you can make in just minutes.

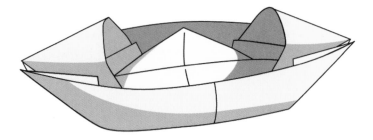

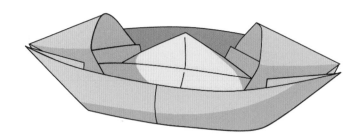

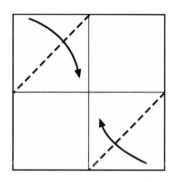

1 Crease both the middle lines and then fold the two corners as shown.

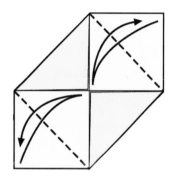

2 Crease the lines on the other two corners.

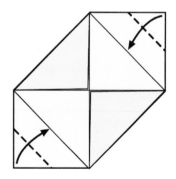

3 Fold the points of the two corners down to the crease lines.

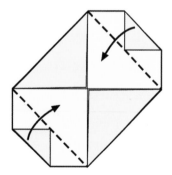

4 Fold along the crease lines.

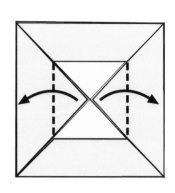

5 Fold the left and right points out as shown.

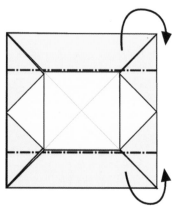

6 Fold the top and bottom to the back side.

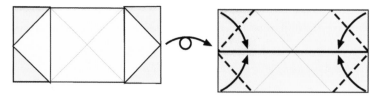

7 Turn the piece over, then fold the four corners.

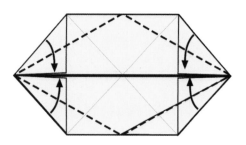

8 Fold along the lines as shown.

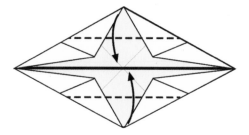

9 Fold down the top and bottom as shown.

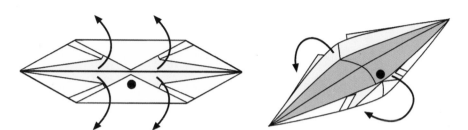

10 Open up and spread out the sides from the very center, making sure you get all the layers, and fold each side behind, essentially turning the piece inside out.

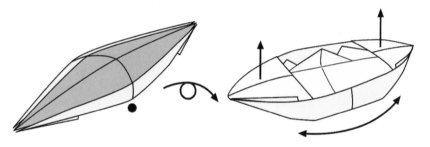

11 Turn the piece over. Lift the left and right sides to create dimension.

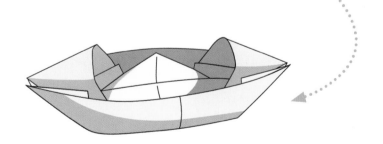

Cherry Blossom

MATERIALS
- 1 sheet
- Scissors
- Pencil (optional)

COLOR SUGGESTIONS

Go outside and find a clean fallen branch, then attach a multitude of these cherry blossoms to it to create an eye-catching centerpiece, perfect for a party.

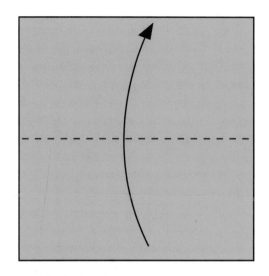

1 Fold in half.

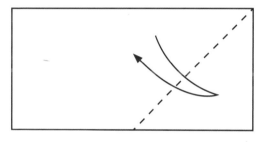

2 Crease the line as shown.

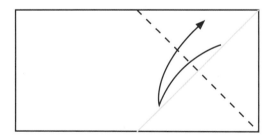

3 Crease the second line as shown.

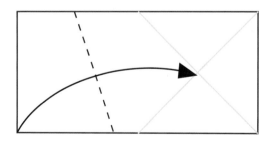

4 Fold the left side as shown.

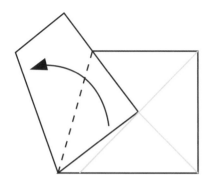

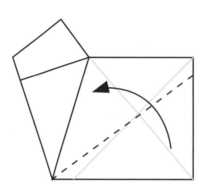

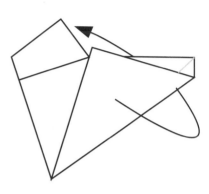

5 Fold back over the previous fold line as shown.

6 Fold the right side as shown.

7 Fold the entire right side behind to the back side.

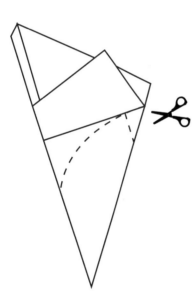

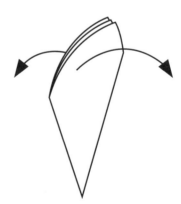

8 Cut all along the dashed lines. You can draw these lines on with a pencil before cutting if you wish.

9 Unfold the paper to see the basic, flat flower shape.

10 Fold each petal segment against the segment next to it until you only have one full petal.

11 Fold the bottom right edge behind to the back side as shown.

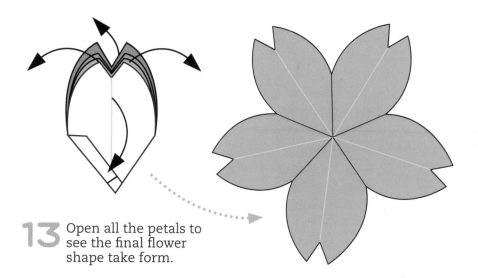

12 Fold the bottom left edge to the front side.

13 Open all the petals to see the final flower shape take form.

Lotus Flower

MATERIAL
- 1 sheet

COLOR SUGGESTIONS

In just a few folds, you can create the most beloved and beautiful flower in the world. You will bring serenity to your living space when you place one of these blooms on your dresser or near a mirror.

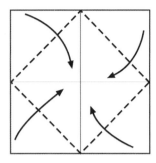 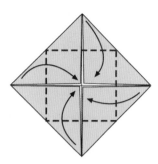 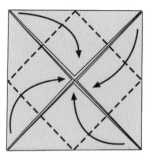

1 Crease both the middle lines and then fold the four corners to the middle.

2 Fold the four new corners to the middle.

3 Fold the four newest corners to the middle one more time.

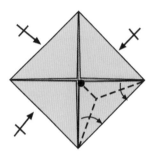 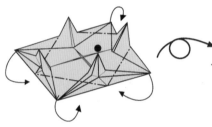 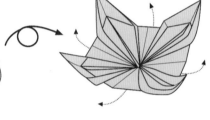

4 Raise each interior point into a vertical position by folding as shown.

5 Once each interior point is sitting straight up, fold each corner under to the back side.

6 Turn the piece over to the back side. The center should be a bit sunken. Fold the little petals (the ones on the underside of the piece as oriented in this illustration) toward the outside so that they are visible between each long petal.

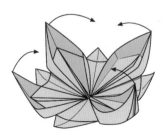

7 Open up and flatten out the corners of each long petal, then carefully press the folds so that the entire flower holds its shape.

Colorful Fish

MATERIAL
- 1 sheet

With this project, you'll soon find yourself basking in the beautiful coral reefs of Japan's waters, swimming alongside fish and rays!

COLOR SUGGESTIONS

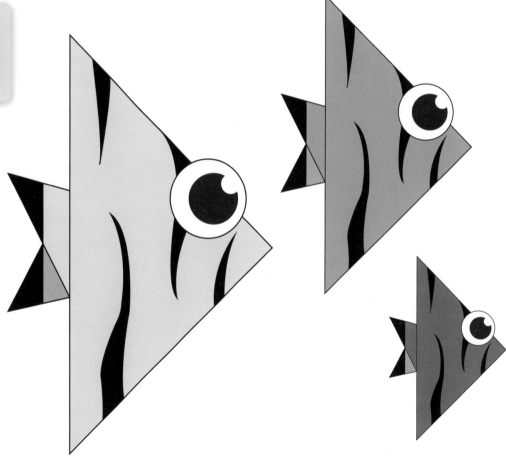

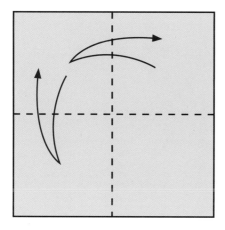

1 Crease the lines as shown.

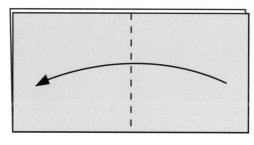

2 Fold the paper in half and then half again, with the patterned side out.

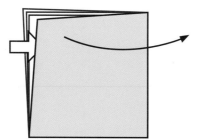

3 Open up the front to the right side to add volume/ create a pocket.

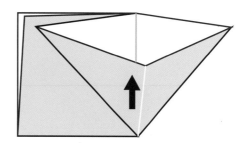

4 Flatten the pocket into a triangle as shown.

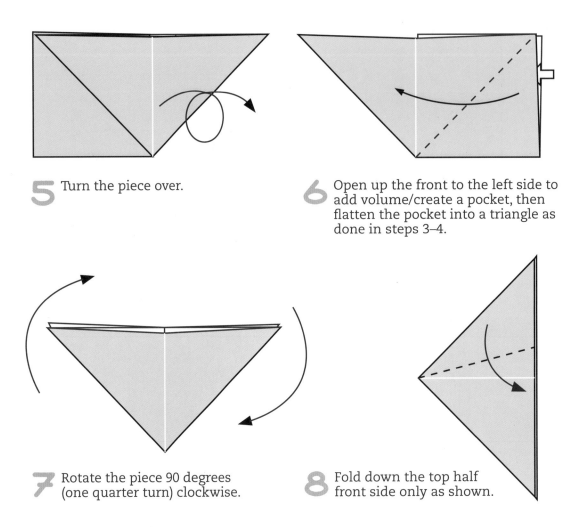

5 Turn the piece over.

6 Open up the front to the left side to add volume/create a pocket, then flatten the pocket into a triangle as done in steps 3–4.

7 Rotate the piece 90 degrees (one quarter turn) clockwise.

8 Fold down the top half front side only as shown.

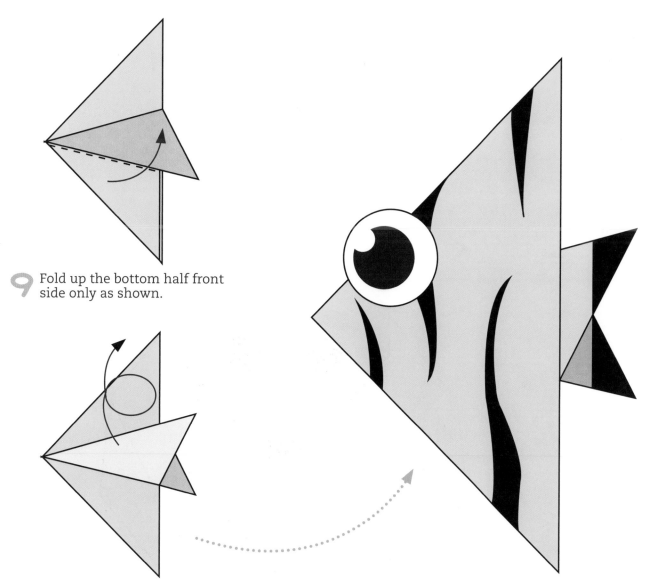

9 Fold up the bottom half front side only as shown.

10 Turn the piece over. Here's your fish!

Raccoon Dog

MATERIAL
• 1 sheet

With their cute little faces, raccoon dogs will charm anyone who sees them. You can make your own adorable companion in a matter of minutes.

COLOR SUGGESTIONS

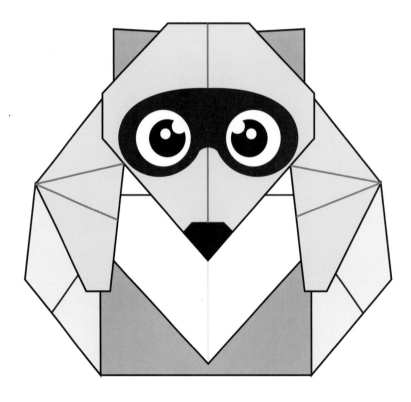

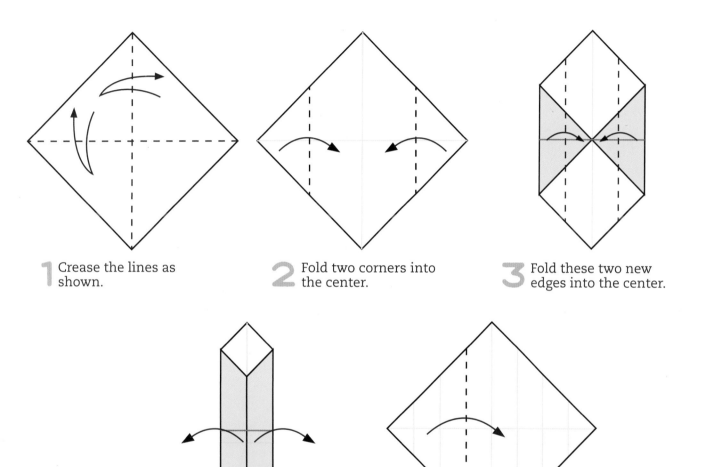

1 Crease the lines as shown.

2 Fold two corners into the center.

3 Fold these two new edges into the center.

4 Unfold the entire sheet.

5 Fold the left side along the indicated line.

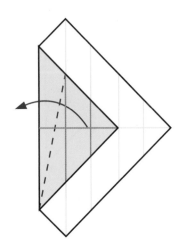

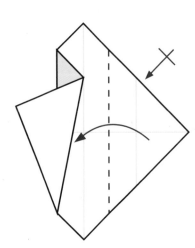

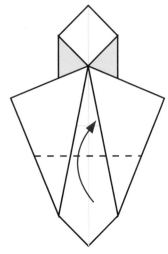

6 Fold back along the diagonal as shown.

7 Repeat steps 5–6 on the right side.

8 Fold up the bottom half.

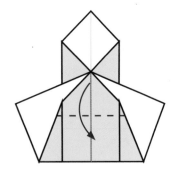

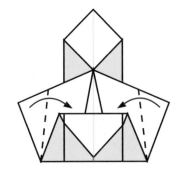

9 Fold the point down as shown.

10 Fold each side in toward the center.

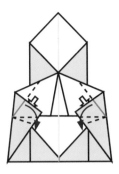

11 Open up each side as shown, fold the outer corners in and down, and then fold the inside edges down to form the front paws.

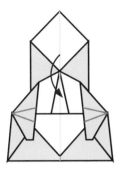

12 Fold the top half down toward the center.

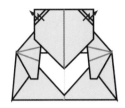

13 Make double folds with the tip of the head on each side to form the ears.

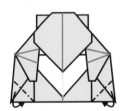

14 Fold the two bottom corners behind to the back side to finish the bottom of the body.

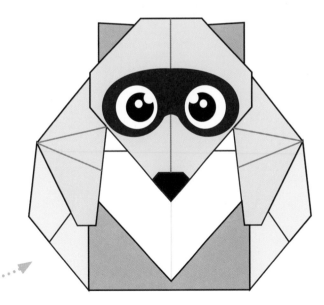

Kimono Crowd

Add some fun designs and colors to your décor with these adorable little figures dressed in traditional Japanese kimonos. Make a whole host of them and affix them to a bicolored string for a festive touch.

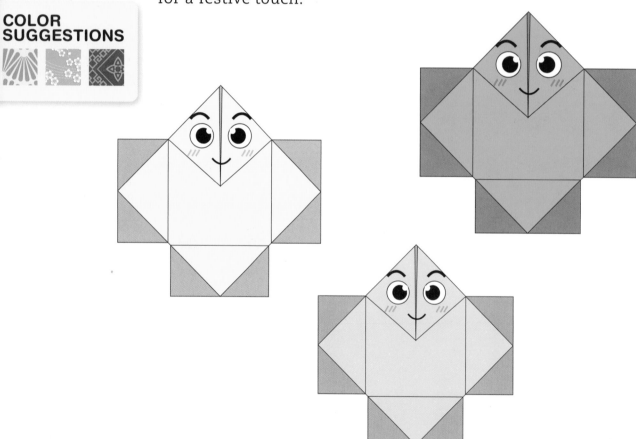

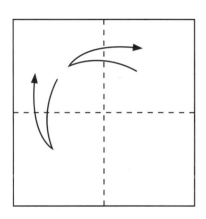

1 Crease the lines as shown.

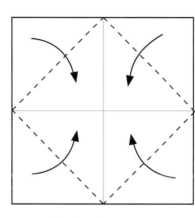

2 Fold the four corners into the center.

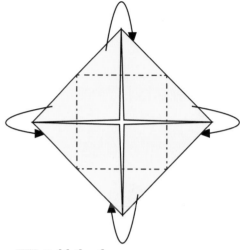

3 Fold the four new corners behind to the back side.

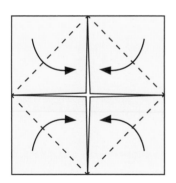

4 Fold the four newest corners into the center.

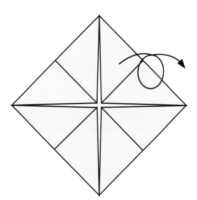

5 Turn the piece over.

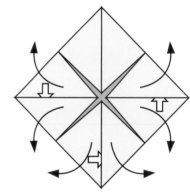

6 Open each of the indicated sides to add volume/create a pocket, then flatten them.

Sumo Wrestlers

Sumo wrestling is a traditional Japanese combat sport. Make two opponents and get them ready for battle!

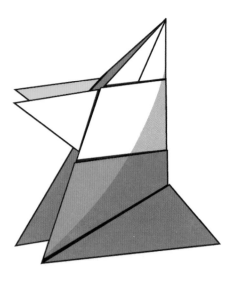

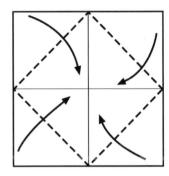 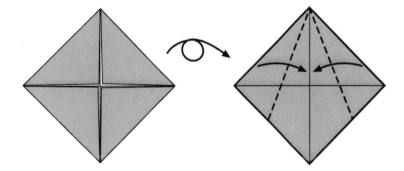

1 Crease both middle lines and then fold the four corners into the center.

2 Turn the piece over. Then fold each side into the center as shown.

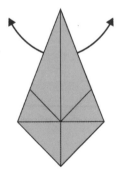 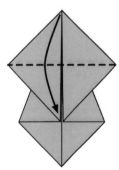

3 Open up the top folds on the back side.

4 Fold the top point down as shown.

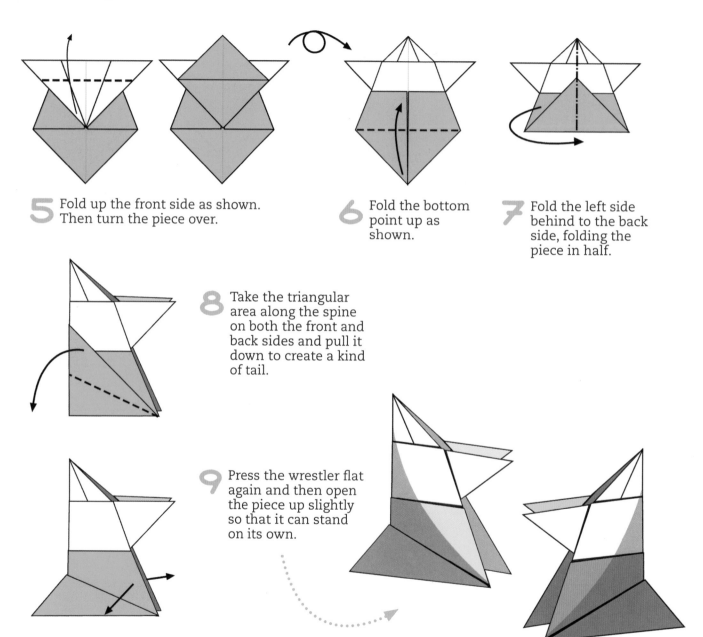

5 Fold up the front side as shown. Then turn the piece over.

6 Fold the bottom point up as shown.

7 Fold the left side behind to the back side, folding the piece in half.

8 Take the triangular area along the spine on both the front and back sides and pull it down to create a kind of tail.

9 Press the wrestler flat again and then open the piece up slightly so that it can stand on its own.

Artistic Boat

MATERIALS
- 1 sheet
- Scissors

COLOR SUGGESTIONS

Here's your ticket to a grand sea voyage on the Pacific Ocean! Choose different papers for each boat to create a whole fleet.

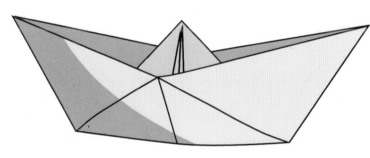

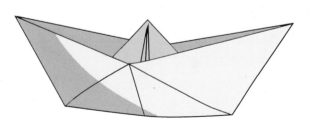

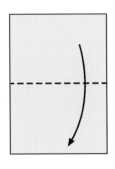

1 Cut a rectangle from the sheet and fold in half. (The long side of the rectangle should be shorter than the width of the original square sheet side; trim it during step 3 if needed.)

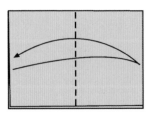

2 Crease the middle line.

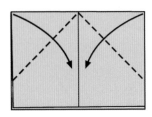

3 Fold the top corners down into the center.

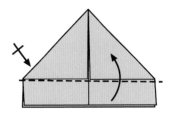

4 Fold up the bottom section on both the front and back sides (separately).

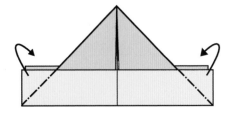

5 Fold the corners, front sides only, behind to the back side.

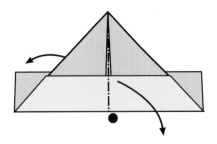

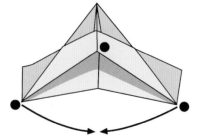

6 Open up the center and join the two sides where marked. Flatten.

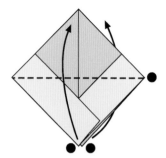

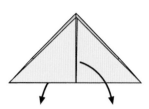

7 Fold up the bottom half on both the front and back sides (separately).

8 Open the piece up as you did in step 6. Flatten.

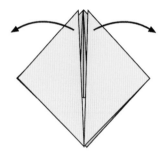

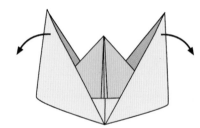

9 Pull each side outward.

10 Open up the bottom of the boat to give it its final shape.

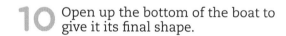

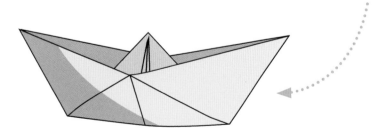

Sly Fox

MATERIAL
- 1 sheet

COLOR SUGGESTIONS

In Japanese culture, the fox is considered one of the most cunning and intelligent animals. Make one and see for yourself!

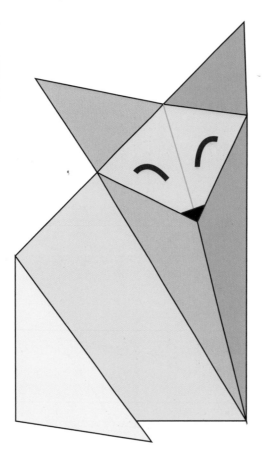

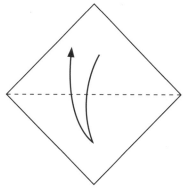

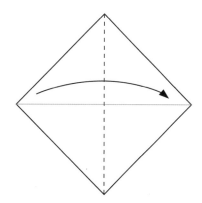

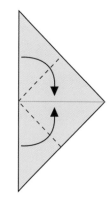

 Crease the line as shown.

Fold in half.

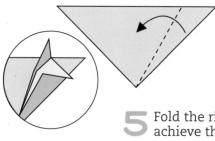 Fold the points into the center as shown to create a square.

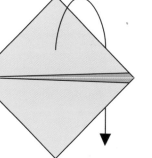 Fold the top half behind to the back side.

Fold the right side to achieve the effect shown.

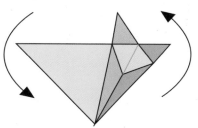 Rotate the piece 90 degrees (one quarter turn) counterclockwise.

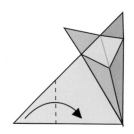 Fold the left side to form the tail.

Fanciful Butterfly

MATERIALS
- 2 sheets
- Tape
- Scrap paper

Create a whirling and colorful decoration with these butterflies! Scatter them along a wall or window to bring some whimsy into your home.

COLOR SUGGESTIONS

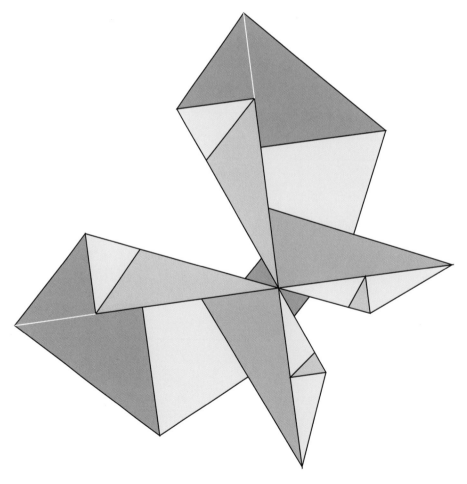

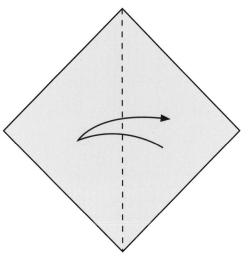

1 Crease the line as shown.

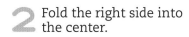

2 Fold the right side into the center.

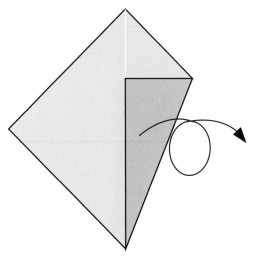

3 Turn the piece over.

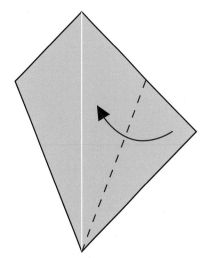

4 Fold the right side into the center.

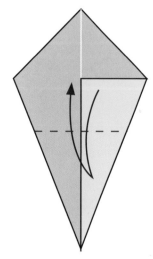

5 Crease the line as shown.

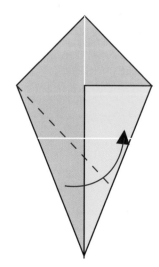

6 Fold the left side as shown.

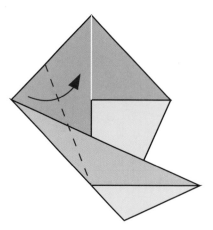

7 Fold the left side into the center.

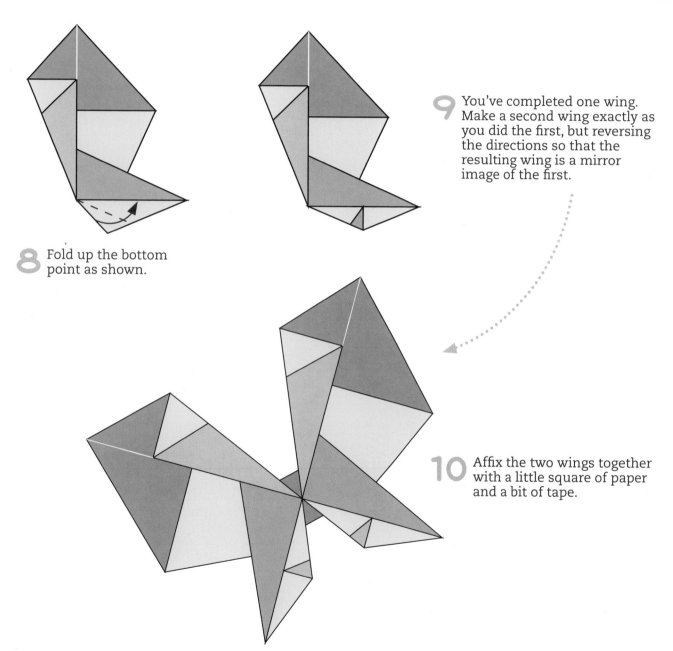

9 You've completed one wing. Make a second wing exactly as you did the first, but reversing the directions so that the resulting wing is a mirror image of the first.

8 Fold up the bottom point as shown.

10 Affix the two wings together with a little square of paper and a bit of tape.

Elegant Lily

This delicate flower will require your concentration, but when it blooms, you'll see that it was worth all the effort.

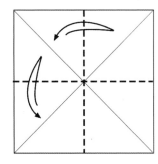

1 Crease all four lines as shown.

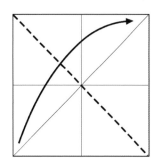

2 Fold in half diagonally.

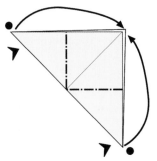

3 Reverse-fold the corners into the inside.

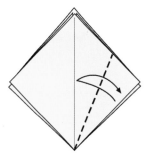

4 Crease the line as shown.

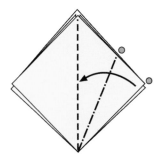

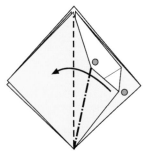

5 Fold the right side (front side only) toward the inside as shown and press the shape flat (see next step).

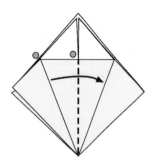

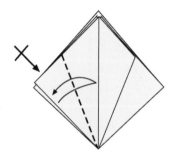

6 Then fold the left center flap to the right as shown.

7 Repeat steps 4–6 with the left side.

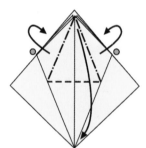

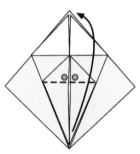

8 Reverse-fold the two sides into the inside as shown, then open up and fold down the front top flap. Flatten it down.

9 Fold the bottom point (front side only) up to the top.

10 Fold in the two center sides as shown. Then turn the piece over.

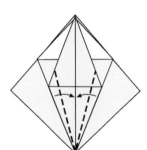

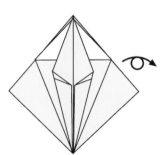

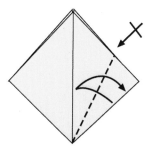

11 Repeat steps 4–10 on the right side.

12 Fold the right half (front side only) to the left and the left half (back side only) to the right (on the back side).

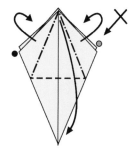

13 Repeat steps 8–10 on both front and back sides.

14 Open up the petals.

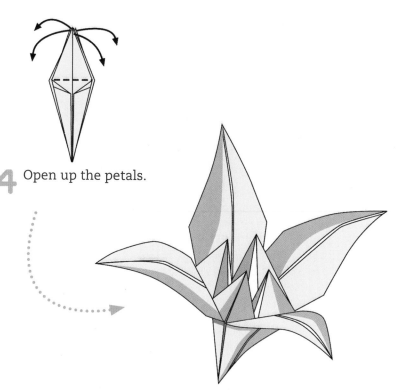

Wise Owl

Everyone knows that owls are wise creatures. By creating one, you will bring wisdom and clear thinking into your home.

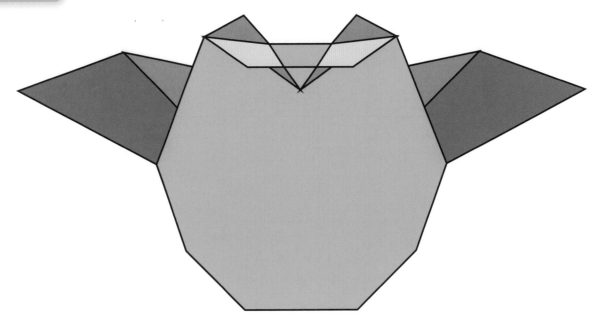

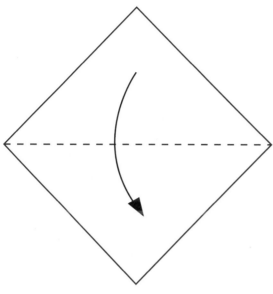

1 Fold the piece in half as shown.

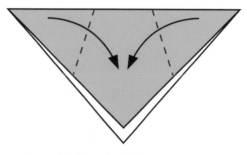

2 Fold first the left corner, then the right corner as shown.

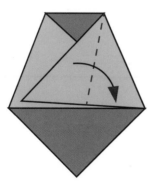

3 Fold the right flap to the right as shown.

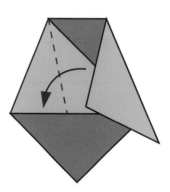

4 Do the same with the left flap.

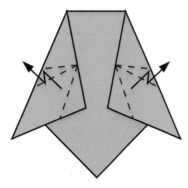

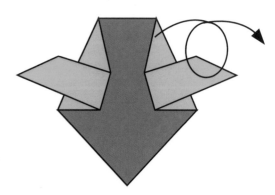

5 Open up the wings by doing a double fold on each side. This is a bit of a difficult fold, so you may have to try it a few times before getting it right. It helps to lift the entire triangle up first to achieve the double fold.

6 Turn the piece over.

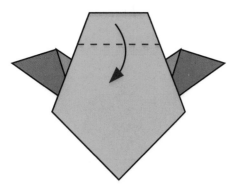

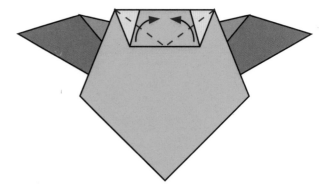

7 Fold the top section down.

8 Fold the two points toward the center as shown, pushing up the two folded triangles to create the ears as you fold toward the center.

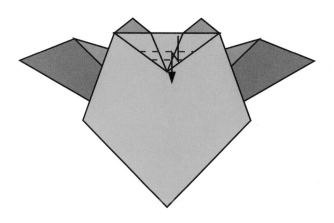

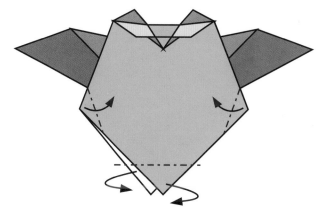

9 Do a double fold to create the beak.

10 Reverse-fold the sides and fold in the bottom to the inside of the owl's body.

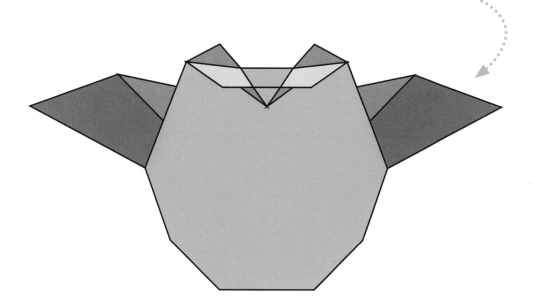

Tranquil Swan

MATERIAL
• 1 sheet

Swans are creatures that just breathe tranquility. Relax while you make one yourself!

COLOR SUGGESTIONS

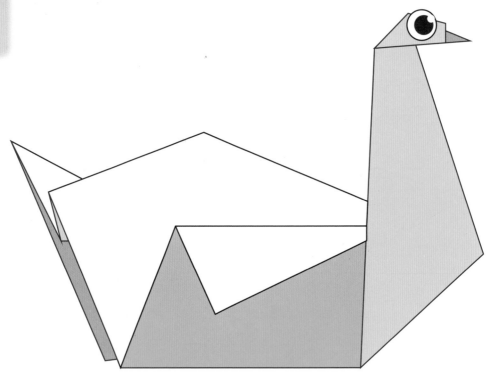

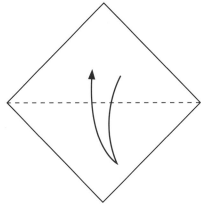

1 Crease the line as shown.

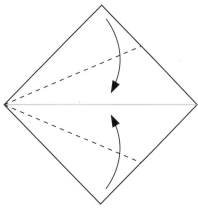

2 Fold the top and bottom points into the center.

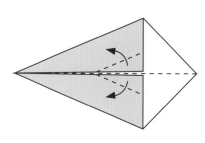

3 Fold the small interior points as shown.

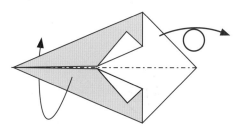

4 Fold the bottom half behind to the back side. Then turn the piece over so that you see the side shown in step 5.

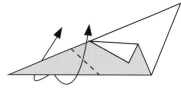

5 Reverse-fold to create the neck.

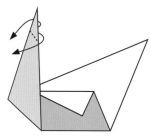

6 Reverse-fold again to create the head.

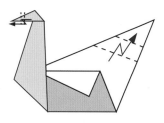

7 Do a double-fold on both the tail and the head to finish the swan.

Serene Bird

MATERIAL
- 1 sheet

**COLOR
SUGGESTIONS**

Make this bird take flight in the form of a mobile or place it along the top of a mirror where you can appreciate its plumage.

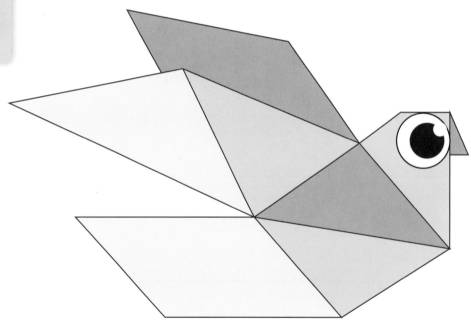

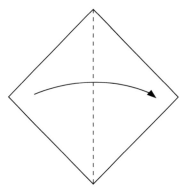

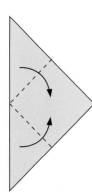

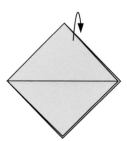

1 Fold in half as shown.

2 Fold the top and bottom points into the center to form a square.

3 Fold the top half behind to the back side to form a triangle.

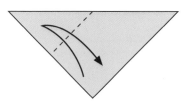

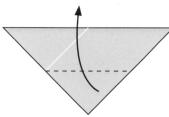

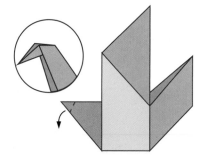

4 Crease the line as shown.

5 Following the edge of the creased line, fold the bottom section up on both the front and back sides (separately).

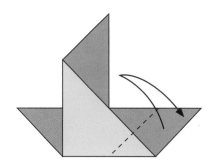

6 Crease the line as shown. Then, on both the front and back sides, pull up the far right tip into a vertical position and allow it to flatten naturally to form the shape shown. These are the wings.

7 Crease the line for the head, then do a reverse fold. Refold the creased line from step 6. You can leave the tail as shown in the illustrations, or you can instead reverse that fold to make the bird's tail dip down instead of up.

57

Message Heart

MATERIAL
- 1 sheet

COLOR SUGGESTIONS

Tuck this meaningful origami into a box of chocolates offered with love on Valentine's Day (or any special occasion).

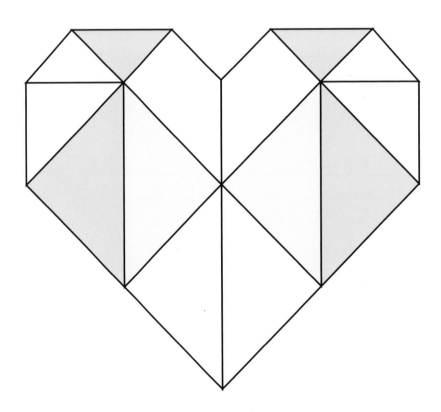

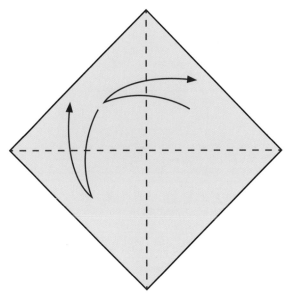

1 Crease the two lines as shown.

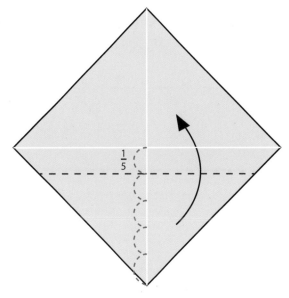

2 Fold up the bottom side at about one-fifth of the way from the centerline.

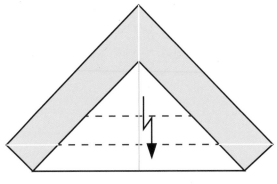

3 Do a double fold.

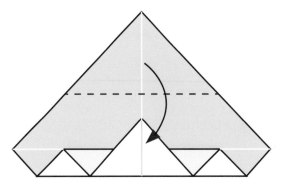

4 Fold the top corner down.

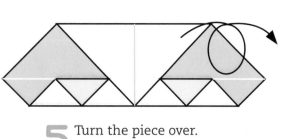

5 Turn the piece over.

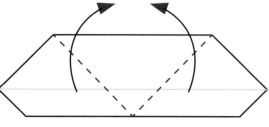

6 Fold up both the left and right sides.

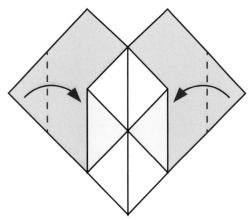

7 Fold the left and right sides toward the center to touch the center points as shown.

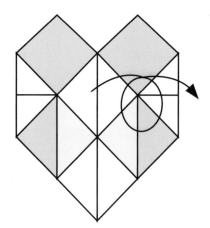

8 Turn the piece over.

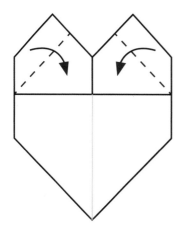

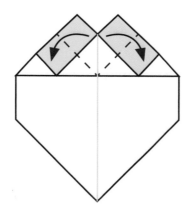

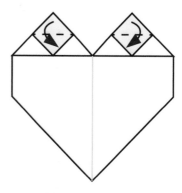

9 Fold down the right side and then the left side as shown.

10 Fold down the top two points as shown.

11 Fold down the top two points as shown one more time.

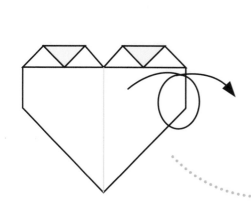

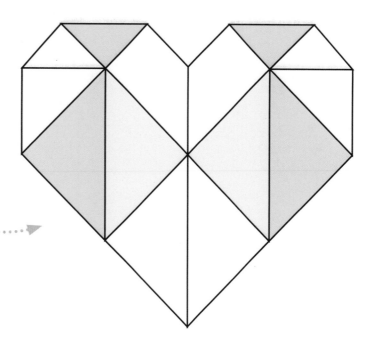

12 Turn the piece over to reveal the finished heart.

Cuddly Dog

MATERIALS

- 1 quarter sheet for each part (head and body)
- Colored dot stickers and/or marker
- Glue or tape

COLOR SUGGESTIONS

Enjoy the process of folding this two-part origami piece. It's a paper companion that will always stay by your side!

Head

1 Fold the top down as shown.

2 Crease the middle line.

3 Fold down the corners to create the ears.

4 Fold up the bottom point on the front side only.

5 Fold up the remaining bottom point behind to the back side.

6 If you want, use colored stickers to create eyes and color in the dog's muzzle with a marker.

Body

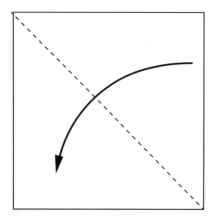

1 Fold in half diagonally.

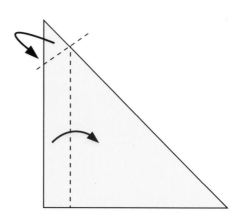

2 Fold as shown. Open up the left side and fold down the top point. Flatten the whole thing.

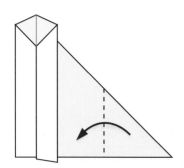

3 Fold the right side to create the tail.

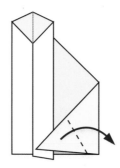

4 Fold the point of the tail to the right as shown.

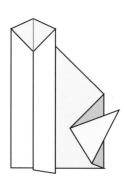

5 Open up and flatten the folds of the tail.

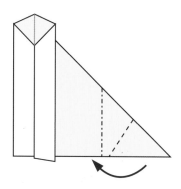

6 Refold the far right fold forward, then fold the left fold behind to the back side.

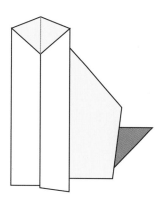

7 The dog's body is done.

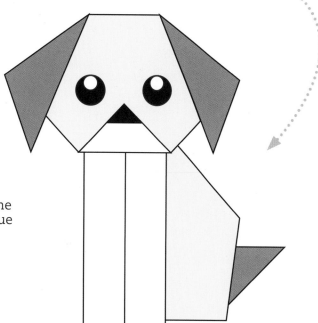

8 Attach the head to the body using a little glue or tape.

Majestic Horse

MATERIAL
- 1 sheet
- Scissors

COLOR SUGGESTIONS

This galloping animal will delight young and old alike. It's a bit of a challenge, but nothing you can't handle!

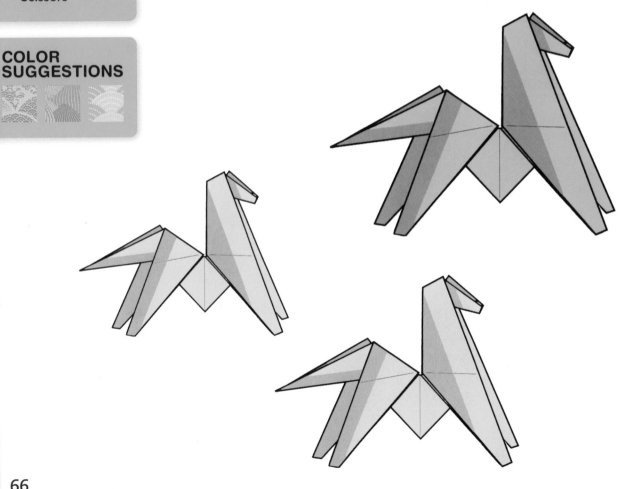

66

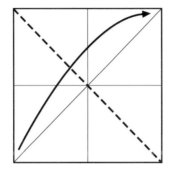

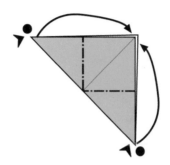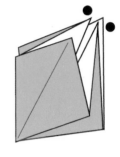

1 Crease all four lines as shown, then fold in half diagonally.

2 Reverse-fold the corners into the inside.

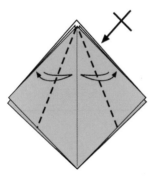

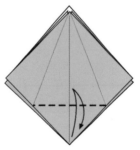

3 Crease the lines as shown on each side on both front and back sides.

4 Crease the line as shown at the bottom on the front side only.

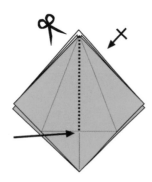

5 On both front and back sides, cut the middle crease line all the way to the bottom fold line as shown.

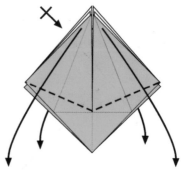

6 Fold down all the points on both front and back sides (four points total).

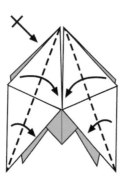

7 Fold each side into the center as shown, on both front and back sides.

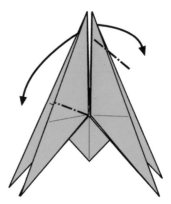

8 Reverse-fold the top right point near the top to create the head. Reverse-fold the top left point near the center to create the tail.

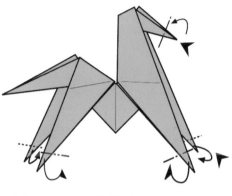

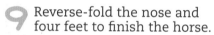

9 Reverse-fold the nose and four feet to finish the horse.

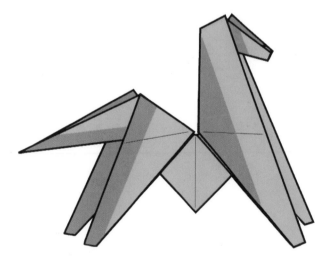

Feisty Fish

Break free of the daily grind little by little by making a whole school of these fun fish.

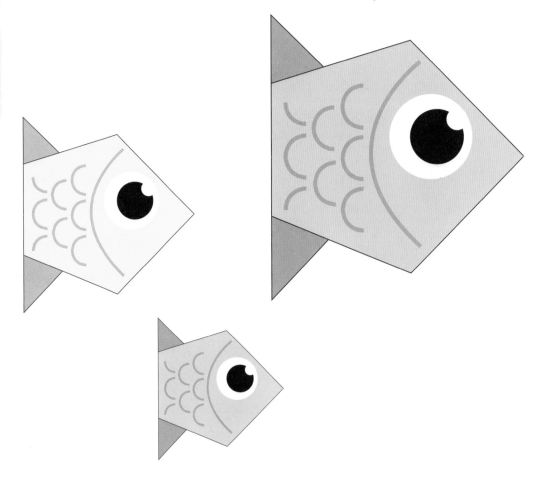

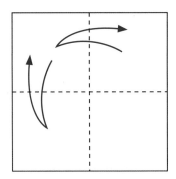

1 Crease the lines as shown.

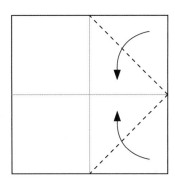

2 Fold the top and bottom right corners into the center.

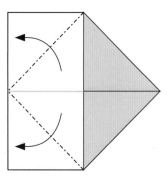

3 Fold the top and bottom left corners into the center, but behind on the back side.

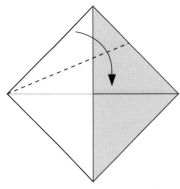

4 Fold down the top into the center as shown. Let the flap at the top come free as shown in step 5.

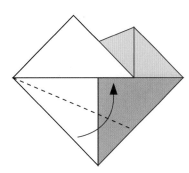

5 Repeat for the bottom half.

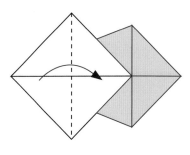

6 Fold the left point into the center as shown.

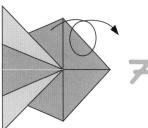

7 Turn the piece over. Your first fish is done!

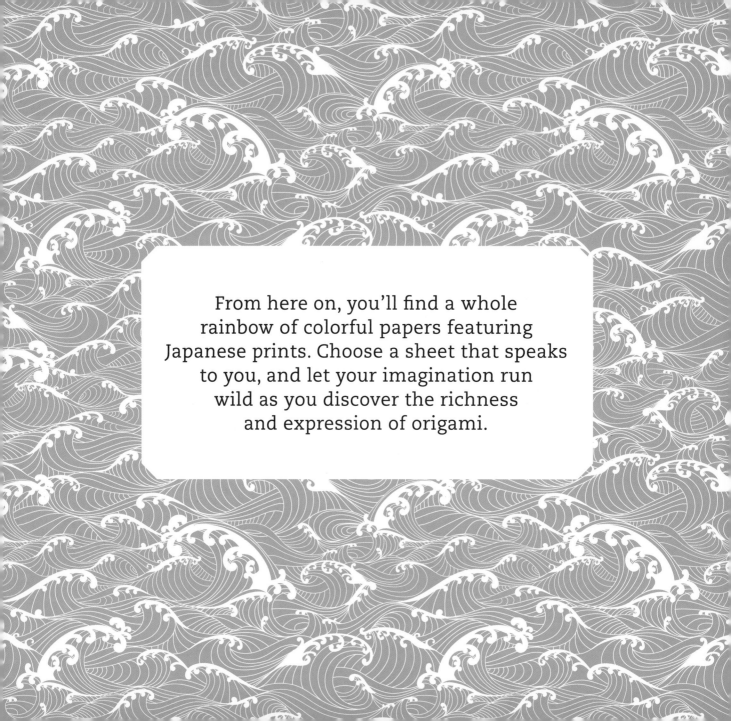

From here on, you'll find a whole rainbow of colorful papers featuring Japanese prints. Choose a sheet that speaks to you, and let your imagination run wild as you discover the richness and expression of origami.

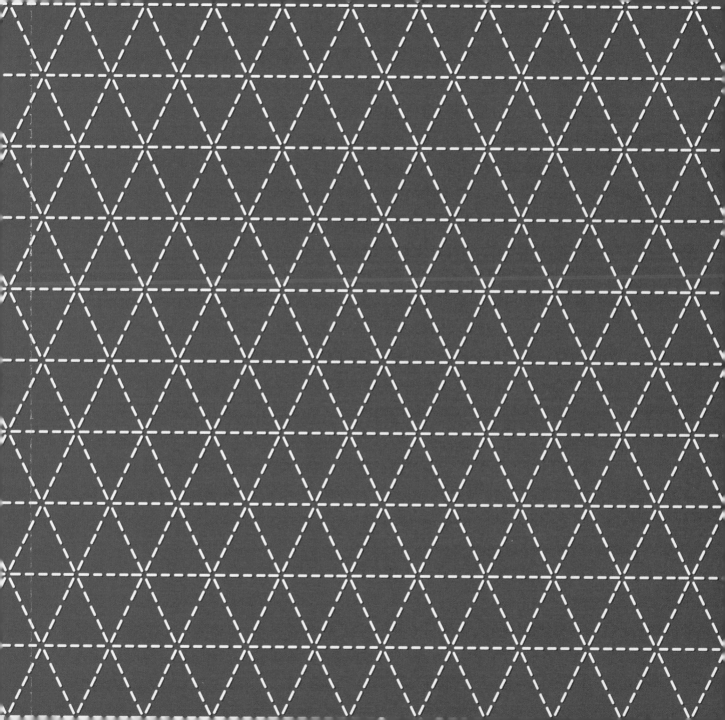

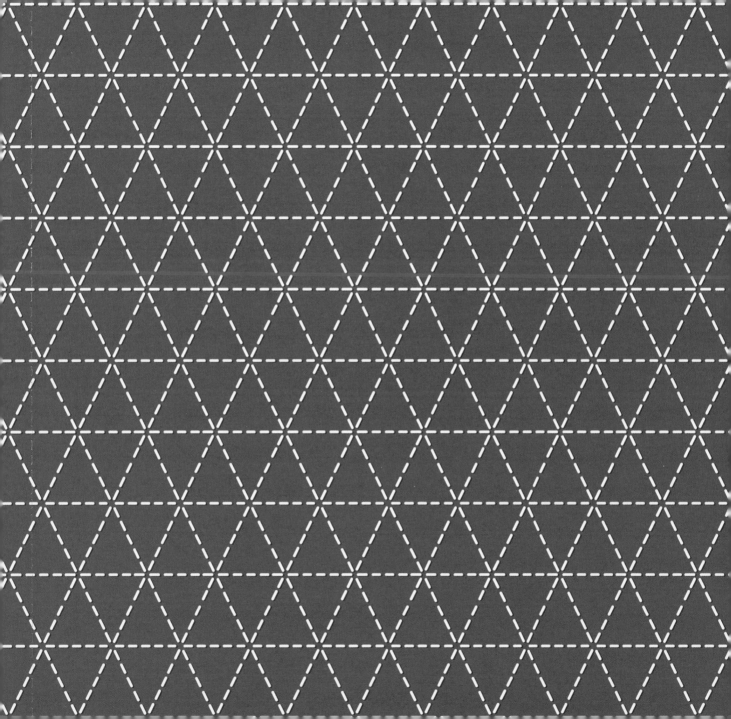

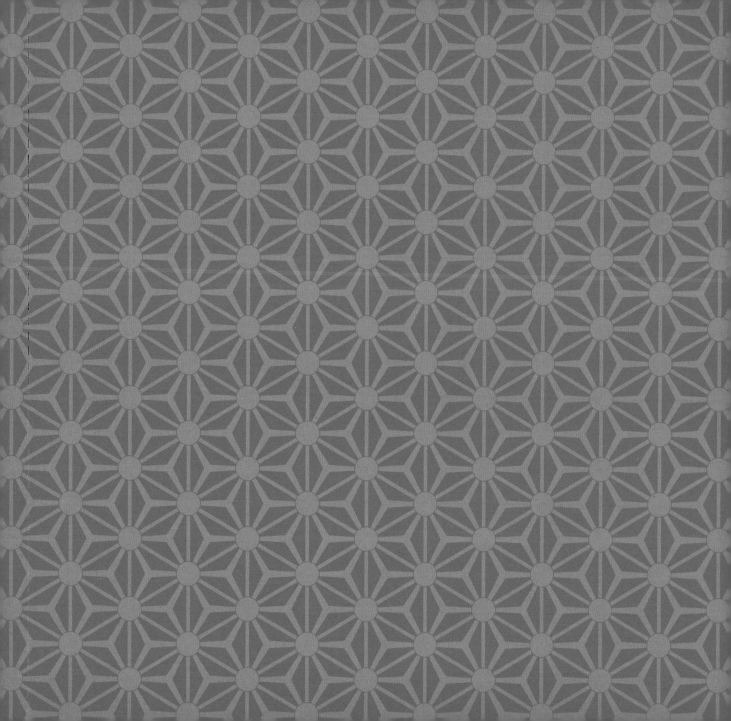

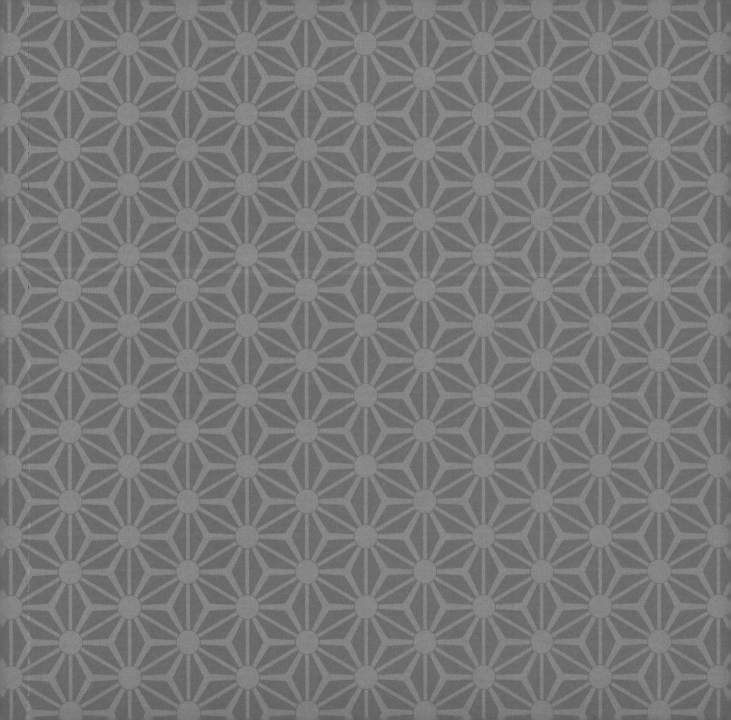

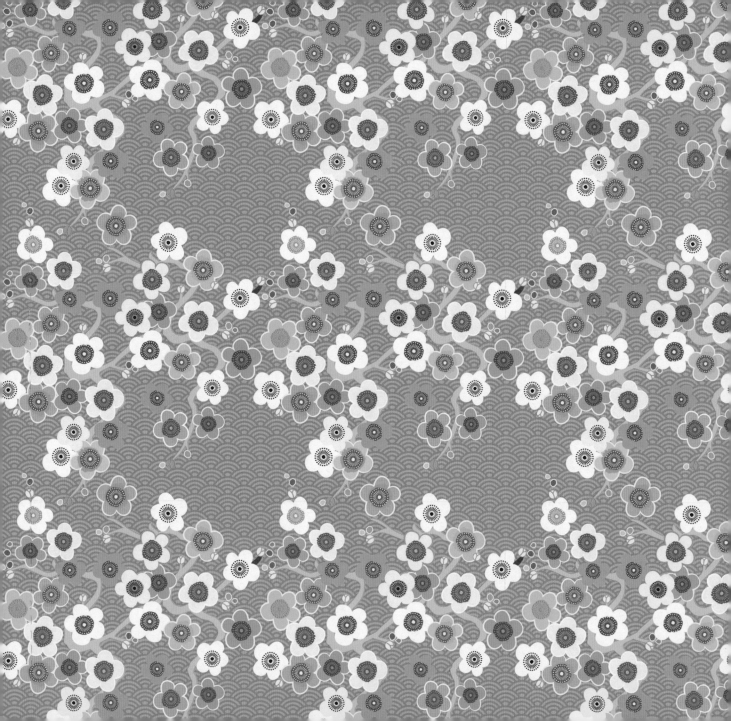

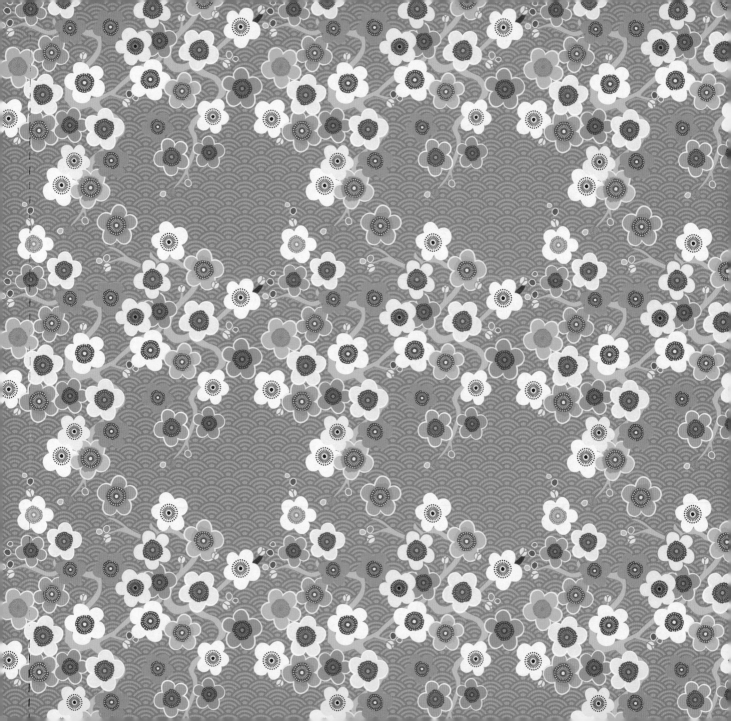

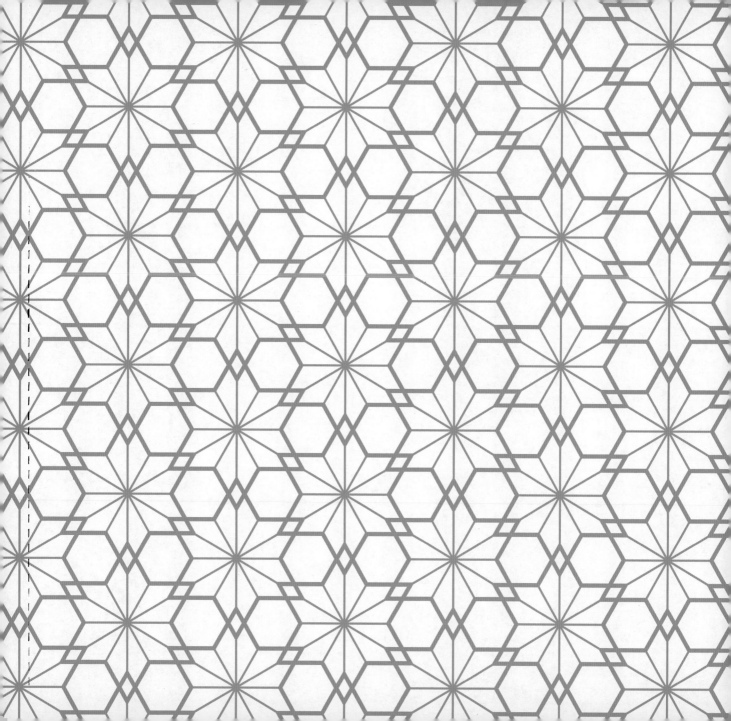

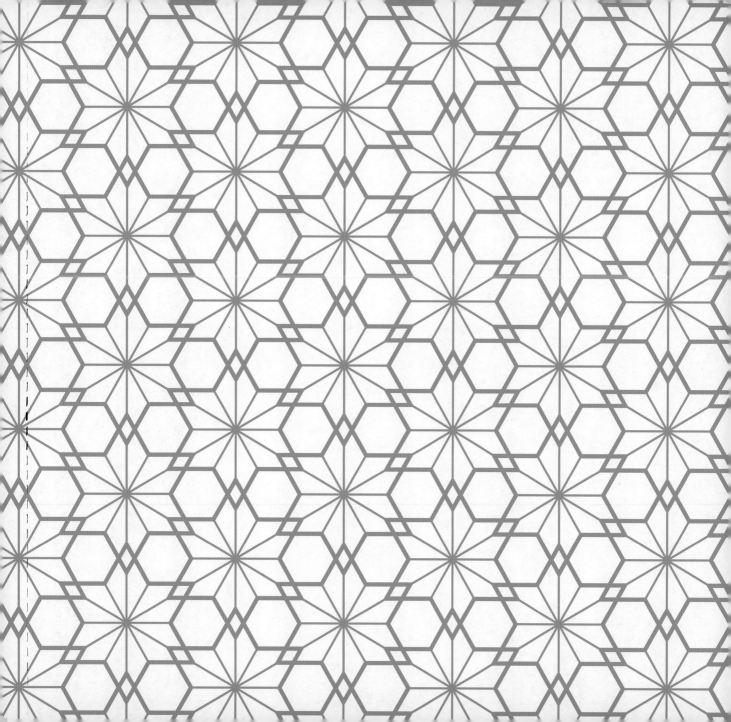

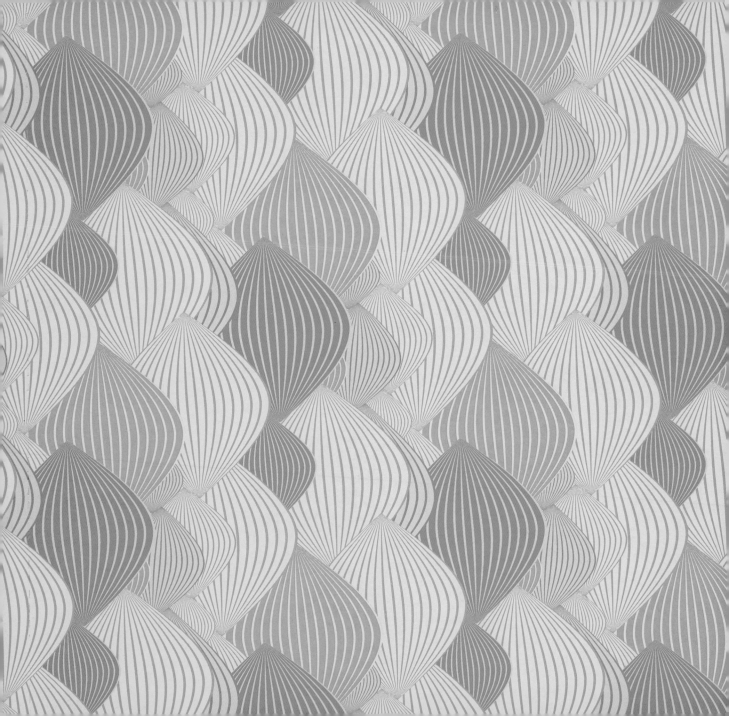

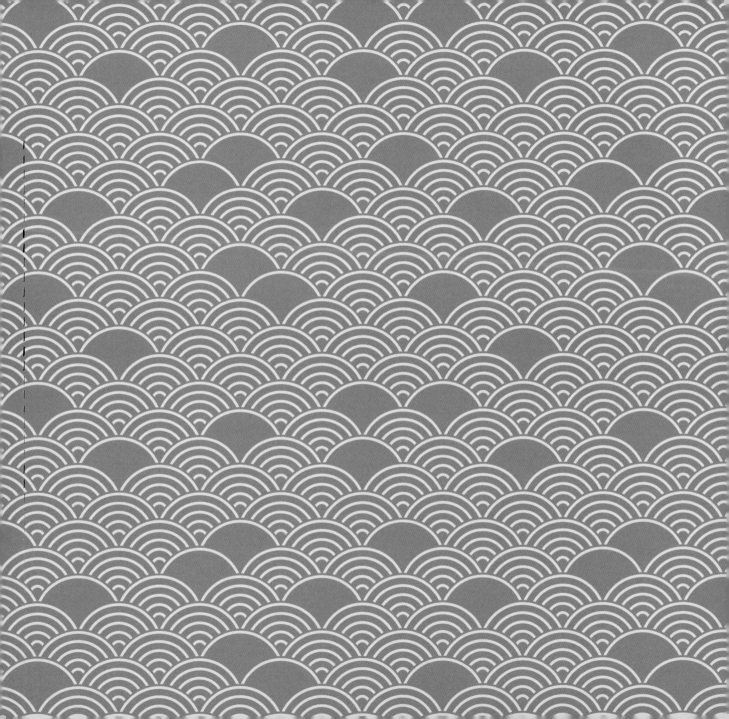

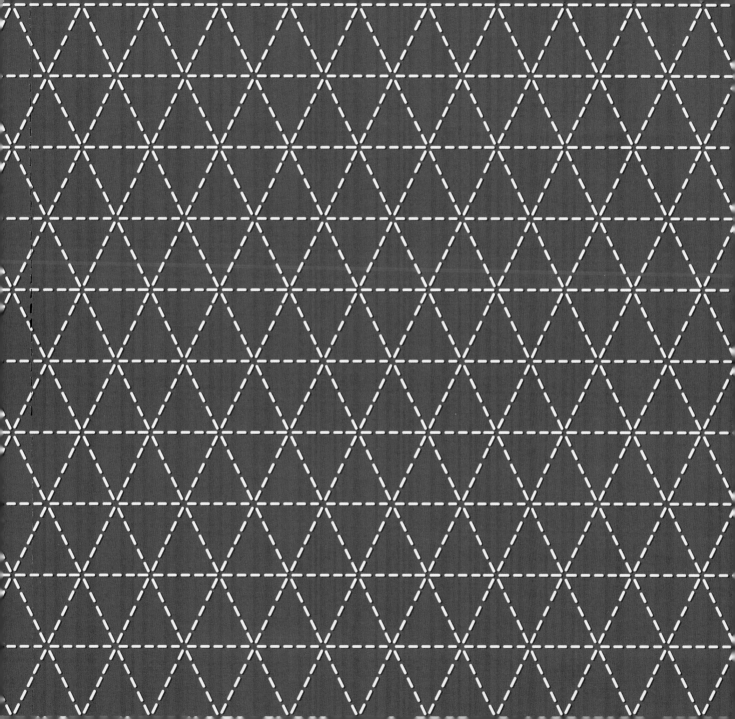

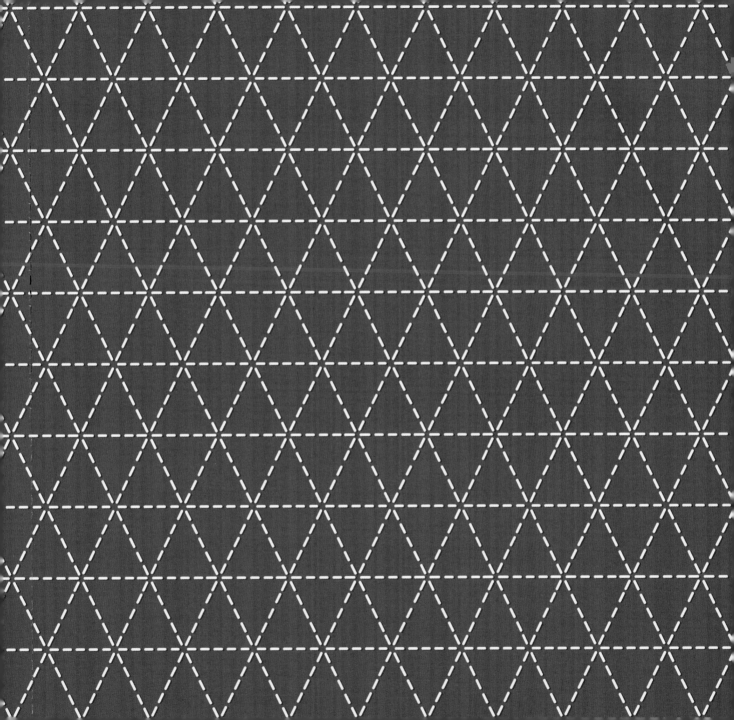